THE Journey OF A Rescued Pit Bull

My Lil Superstar D'Angelo

by Kathy Qualy

Based on a true story

All proceeds from the sale of this book will benefit animal welfare and rescue.

The Journey of a Rescued Pit Bull, My Lil Superstar D'Angelo
Copyright ©2016 Kathy Qualy

ISBN: 978-0-9978721-1-8

Illustrations: Maya Klauber: mklaub@gmail.com
Book design: Peggy Nehmen, n-kcreative.com
Photos: Kathy Qualy
Photos on pages 51, 53, 64: ©Anthony Costello Blue Nose Studios

For information about custom editions, special sales,
or corporate purchases, please contact: pitbullsuperstar@gmail.com

Printed in the United States of America

Published by Qualy Press, St. Louis, MO
www.pitbullsuperstar.org

 @dangelo_nybc

 Pit Bull Superstar D'Angelo

 New York Bully Crew | D'Angelo's Story

Dedication

To those involved in animal welfare and rescue...
May your passion remain unwavering despite
the tremendous heartache that is a by-product
of your inspiring work.

To all animal foster parents...
You do not foster because it is easy to let them go;
you foster because it is easier than letting them die.
When the sadness sets in, remember how important
your role is in the rescue and rehabilitation of dogs
and other abandoned animals. You have remarkably
impacted the world.

To our precious D'Angelo...
I am continually astonished by your will to live,
amazed by your ability to forgive, and encouraged
by your enormous and tender heart. The way you
love every person despite the abuse you
endured gives me hope.

I am D'Angelo

Lucky Dog

I am D'Angelo, which in Italian means, "from the angels." My life is almost perfect now. I am the luckiest dog alive, but it wasn't always like this. Today, I live in a nice house with my human parents and three "fursisters." I am the only brother. We all get along great, which is amazing, since we all came from different places and at different times. At first, we didn't feel like a family, but after a while, the four of us bonded and became what my mom calls "a pack." We are all pit bulls or pitbull mixes, even though we don't look anything alike.

I am the largest dog, weighing in at eighty-two pounds, which is miraculous considering the condition I was in not so long ago. Healthy food and long pack walks helped me become stronger and more confident.

My human parents are wonderful people, and they really love us, which is also incredible because not everyone even likes pit bulls. Most people don't know much about our breed and think all pit bulls are mean and vicious. This is called stereotyping, and it upsets my mom, dad and other pit bull owners, who think we have sweet dispositions. Mom explained that some people train pit bulls to fight other dogs so the cruel owners can gamble and win money. I know this is true because in my early years I was one of those dogs.

It's hard to remember my past because my life today is so different. I love my pack and we are always tumbling around and playing. We are learning many new things, especially how to have good manners. I am taking advanced obedience classes with my mom because I am training to be a therapy dog. This is an honor because not all dogs are accepted into this program.

One of the first requirements for therapy dogs is having just the right temperament. When my training is completed, I will spend time in hospitals and other rehabilitation facilities visiting people who are sick or injured. My mom says that touching dogs makes sick people feel better, so I'm happy to be learning to become a Therapy Touch dog. I want to comfort people, as I was comforted when I was sick. I want to inspire everyone to make the world a better place for both humans and animals.

My "Ruff" Start

I never expected my life to be as wonderful as it is now. I wasn't born into a life of luxury with parents who loved me and took care of me. I thought a life like that was a fairy tale and it could never happen to me. In fact, I was taught from the very beginning not to expect much out of life. My dog mother told me life was going to be tough and I guess she knew from her own experience what the world was like for pit bulls.

I had the feeling that my brothers and sisters and I were not her first litter, because she was tired all the time. She had to work hard to feed everybody, because there were so many of us, and we were always hungry. After about a month, I noticed there were fewer puppies clamoring for food. I wondered where they had gone until the day I was also taken away from my dog mother.

Being separated from my first family was hard and I cried because I didn't want to leave. My dog mother was the only one who took care of me and fed me and I liked playing around in the grass with my brothers and sisters. I didn't know where I was going, which was scary. Even scarier was the large man with his rough hands who picked me up and carried me off. He tucked me under his enormous arm like a football and very quickly walked away. He dumped me in the back of a van with some other puppies that looked like my brothers and sisters, but I could tell they were strangers.

The Fighting Life

My new owner already kept a large group of dogs, so I couldn't imagine why he would want more. It turned out he was training us to fight. I didn't know it then, but I found out later that pit bulls are supposed to be good fighting dogs. Our abusive, greedy owners trained us to fight each other so they could gamble and win money. I didn't like fighting at all, but I didn't want my owner to be angry with me, so I tried very hard to learn to fight. Whatever it takes to be a good dog fighter, I guess I didn't have it in me because I kept losing. My owner wasn't very happy and when I lost, he would get extremely angry. Then he would give me another chance to redeem myself, but I never improved. He finally just gave up hoping I would ever win a fight and washed his hands of me. That meant he wasn't going to feed me anymore because he didn't want to "throw good money after bad." I didn't know what that saying meant, but I did know that every day I was becoming hungrier and weaker.

Sometime later, my owner wrapped me up in a tattered, old blanket and took me for a long ride. He pulled me out of the car, dumped me on the grass in front of a house, and drove away. I don't know how long I lay there. I was too weak to raise my head to look around or bark. I must have fallen asleep because a man woke me up when he tried to pick up the blanket. He must have thought the blanket was trash and wasn't expecting to find a dog inside, especially one that looked as bad as I did. I tried to wag my tail but didn't even have the strength to move it.

The stranger left me there and went back inside the house. After a while, a car drove up and two policemen got out. They tried to give me water but I couldn't lift my head to drink it. The officers wrapped the blanket around me and put me in the back seat of their patrol car. I remember that they were very gentle and kind and then I fell asleep again.

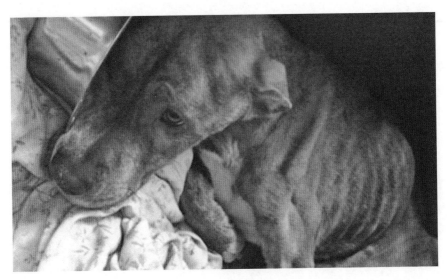

D'Angelo, rescue day.

Rescued

The two officers drove to the police station and carried me inside. People gathered around to look at me, but I was too weak to even notice their presence. I don't remember how long I stayed at the police station before a nice lady named Jade came to get me. Two policemen helped her carry me to her car, and we went for another ride to a place called Grady Animal Hospital. I had never been to an animal hospital before and had no idea what to expect, but I was too sick to even be afraid. I didn't realize I was dying of starvation. I weighed only 30 pounds, yet I was a full grown dog.

There was a nice man at the hospital whose name was Dr. Mark. He knew what was wrong with me the minute he looked at me and immediately began to get some nourishment into my body. Dr. Mark was a veterinarian, a doctor who takes care of animals instead of people. He was very worried about me that first night, not sure I would live until morning, but somehow I did. Dr. Mark saved my life, but it would be quite a while before I was healthy again.

Soon after I arrived at Grady Animal Hospital, a man came to visit me. He had heard about me from the people at the police station. His name was Craig and he was the nicest human I had ever met in my life. He stayed with me the whole time I was there and kept telling me I was going to be alright. He called me "My Lil Superstar D'Angelo."

Craig comforted me through my worst days, making me feel safe and secure. He scratched

D'Angelo near death, two hours after rescue.

my head and petted me. When I got a little stronger, I would paw at his hands so he
wouldn't stop. It was the first time in my life I
could remember ever feeling really safe. At first,
I didn't understand why a total stranger would
care so much about me. I owe my life to Craig
and everyone who was part of my rescue team.

My Foster Family

When I was released from the hospital, I was still in pretty bad shape. Dr. Mark said it would be very expensive to keep me in the Grady Animal Hospital. I had no idea what would happen to me now that I had to leave, but Craig turned out to be my angel when he took me to his home.

That's when I realized why he had helped to take care of me. Craig loved all dogs, especially pit bulls. *Nineteen* dogs lived at Craig's house—more than I had ever seen in one place. Craig owned ten of them and was a foster parent to the rest until they could find "furever" families to adopt them. There was even a mama dog with some of her puppies; they had been neglected and abandoned as well. Some of the other dogs were injured or sick and needed a place to heal and grow stronger. If we had not had a foster home to go to, there is no telling what would have happened to us. Dogs stayed at Craig's until they were strong and healthy enough to be adopted by a family or placed at the rescue facility.

All of these dogs seemed happy and well fed. They were so glad to see Craig when we walked through the door and they were very curious about me. They wanted to play, but I was still too exhausted to move around. Craig gently placed me on a warm blanket spread across a cozy bed. He held my head up to feed me little tiny bits of food from a spoon. He was a kind and patient caregiver, which made me feel so happy.

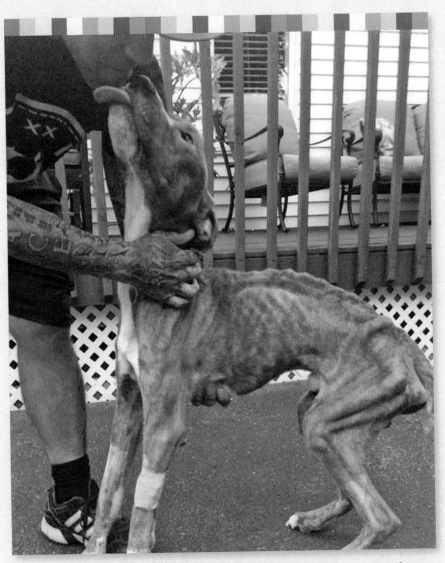

One week after rescue, D'Angelo finally able to stand
with Craig Field's help.

A Second Chance

I had such a rough first night that the following morning, Craig had to take me back to the animal hospital. I don't know how long I remained there because I slept most of the time. Everyone was very attentive. They scratched my head and kept saying, "Hang on, My Lil Superstar." Craig continued to stay by my side, telling me I was a very good boy and that I was going to get better. I knew I was very lucky to have been given a second chance, so I ate all of my food and wagged my tail when I had the strength. I still didn't have any idea why people would be so compassionate to a sick dog.

After a few days I began to feel a little better and Craig took me to his house to be with his pack, which is like a dog family. Being part of a pack made me feel secure and confident. He taught me how I was expected to behave and interact with the other dogs.

Many of us had to learn dog manners since we had no previous training. Craig taught us how to get along with other dogs, as well as people. This was especially true if we had been abused, homeless or left roaming the streets. I had a lot to learn because I had never been trained to do anything but fight. That was not a good way to grow up, but now that I had been given a second chance, I hoped my future would be better and that I could do something to help others.

The New York Bully Crew (NYBC)

I was still pretty sick when Craig took me to his house the second time. He knew how to take care of sick dogs. He again fed me little bits of food with a spoon. He held my head up to feed me because I had not yet regained my strength. After a while, food started tasting good to me, and my appetite improved. I was really happy about this because I had always loved to eat. Every day I got a little stronger, and slowly, I began to feel like my old self again.

I loved my new pack. Everyone was very nice to me while I was getting better, but my doggie friends Dante, Marshall, and Matti were my favorites.

I especially loved the cute little puppies that crawled on my bed and showered me with puppy kisses. We played inside the house and outside in the yard and went on many pack walks together. Craig trained us to behave especially well on our walks. Sometimes, we would see people staring at us as we walked by, and I wondered what they must have been thinking. There were so many of us on leashes walking in our own lanes. Every once in a while, Craig would say something to one of us. He always called us by our names. When he said, "Good boy, D'Angelo. You're doing a great job!" I felt very proud of myself.

Craig talked to us all the time. He told us all about a place called the New York Bully Crew that he had founded in 2010. It was an animal rescue place for dogs like us that needed a fresh start in life. When I became strong enough, I would be able to go there to live temporarily until I was adopted by a "furever" family.

D'Angelo getting stronger.

The dogs that live at the Bully Crew are loved and cared for by many wonderful people who love dogs. They all have one or more dogs of their own. They sometimes even bring their dogs to work. The staff at New York Bully Crew and all rescue crews depend on volunteers who spend time with the dogs and help train them to become more adoptable. At first, I had no idea that being loved and exercised made dogs better behaved. However, over time, I began to see how I was changing—feeling safer and more confident than I had ever felt before.

Finally, I was strong enough to be housed at NYBC! Craig told us that if we learned to be around people and play well with other dogs, we would have a better chance of being adopted. We certainly had many chances to play with other dogs. There were more than seventy dogs at the Bully Crew when I went to live there and many more dogs being cared for in foster homes. It was here that I realized a rescue is not complete until a dog finds its permanent "furever" home.

Some volunteers donated their time to walk us and play with us. Other volunteers contributed money to pay for food, treats, medicine, vet bills, blankets, towels, and the many other things a rescue operation requires to take care of so many dogs. Craig and his staff spend lots of time trying to match each dog with the perfect human family.

I had no idea how much work it took to find the right match between dogs and humans. I learned that every family who wants to adopt one of us must fill out an application, which allows NYBC to get to know them. The Bully Crew staff screens the family and does a home inspection to ensure this will be a good environment in which the dogs can thrive. That's how I found my family, or how they found me.

One day, Craig told me a very special family was driving a long way to meet me and they wanted to adopt me. I knew all about adoption because everybody at the Bully Crew discussed it. I was really hopeful that someday it would happen to me! Despite my "ruff" start, for the first time in a long time, I hoped that I might become a part of a family.

This family really wanted me and they were driving over a thousand miles to come get me and take me home with them. I already knew that some dogs were not so lucky and had to wait a very long time to be adopted. They stay in shelters like the Bully Crew and watch other dogs go off to their "furever" homes. I was thrilled and could hardly wait to meet my new humans.

My "Furever" Family

It must take a long time to drive a thousand miles because I felt like I was waiting endlessly for my new family to arrive. I was nervous the day I was to meet them. What if they didn't like me? Everyone at the shelter made sure I looked my best for the introduction. They gave me a bath and put a cute scarf around my neck. Boy, did I feel handsome!

My new family finally walked in the door, and I was surprised to see that they had a pretty, pint-sized dog with them. They had brought her all the way from Missouri to New York to meet me. Her name was Miss Piggy, and she was going to be my new "fursister."

Miss Piggy was very shy, having also experienced a rocky past. She had been used as bait for a dog-fighting ring even though she was only a puppy and had never wanted to be a fighting dog. After she was adopted, it took her a long time to feel safe and comfortable around people and other dogs. Because my family was so loving and patient with Miss Piggy, she eventually regained her trust in humans and other dogs, although she will always have a struggle with her past issues.

My new parents brought her along so we could get to know each other for a few days before we traveled home. I thought it was a good idea, especially when I learned there were two other dogs waiting for me at home. My new pack would be made up of three pit bulls or pit-bull mixes (I am a purebred pit bull), and one black mutt. That's a lot of dogs, but I liked being around a lot of dogs.

My new family was a very intentional concerning my introduction to Miss Piggy. They wanted to make sure we had time to get to know each other and feel comfortable together. Sometimes this process takes a long time, especially for abused dogs. In our case, it only took a few days.

The first thing we did was take walks several times per day, which gave us plenty of time to play and sniff. We began the drive back home to Missouri to my new home. We spent a long time in the car, which helped us get to know each other even better. Miss Piggy and I snuggled most of the way home. We even spent two nights in a hotel so we could learn to live in the same space with each other. I loved Miss Piggy right away. She was so sweet and small, and I felt it was my job to protect her. I think she sensed that because she began to trust me and feel very safe and secure around me.

When we finally arrived in Missouri, I was introduced to Daisy and Nestle, who were my other "fursisters." It turns out that all four of us had similar challenging and abusive backgrounds.

Daisy had been rescued from a high-kill shelter in Missouri where she did not have much time left to live if she wasn't adopted. The shelter was so crowded with dogs of all kinds that needed homes that it was running out of room. The shelter simply couldn't save all of those dogs, so Daisy was lucky to be adopted by our wonderful parents.

Daisy's coat is a beautiful, shiny black. When I first saw her, I thought she was one of the prettiest dogs I had ever seen and was surprised to find out that not everyone wants to adopt a black dog.

Nestle had been abandoned by her owner and was found wandering the streets. She also ended up in a shelter before my family fell in love and rescued her.

It didn't take long for my new "fursisters" to accept me and for me to feel comfortable with them. We spent hours and hours on pack walks until I felt I was part of the family. My parents know a lot about dogs, especially shelter dogs. I was the sixth one they had adopted. They knew how to be very patient with us because sometimes it takes a while for shelter dogs to trust people again.

Even though I had a difficult start in life, I learned to trust people very quickly. I always appreciated my second chance and know my "fursisters" did as well. My parents also knew how important it was to take us for walks several times a day because we loved being outside and were better behaved when we had lots of exercise.

The past has begun to fade from my memory because I am in such a loving and nurturing environment. My parents are so good to me—to all of us—it is hard to remember a time when I was not well cared for. In my new home I am never hungry or lonely. We have wonderful food, lots of attention, and a big backyard with a fence where we can play safely outside. Inside the house, we are only allowed to lie on chairs covered with blankets. We know which chairs are ours and which chairs are off limits. We spend time in the house, in the yard, and even in the car when we take family trips. All of us are snugglers and, in winter, we cuddle in a furry pile to stay warm. Ms. Piggy is my favorite snuggle buddy, and we spend a lot of time together. She is so darned cute!

My life is good, but it is about to get even better. My mom surprised me when she told me I was going to train to be a therapy dog.

Miss Piggy gives D'Angelo a big doggie hug.

Becoming A Therapy Dog

Becoming a therapy dog requires difficult training but my mom is very patient while she works with me. The most basic part of this training is learning to be comfortable around people because there are lots of people in hospitals and other places I might go. Many of the people will probably want to pet me, which is great because that is something I love. As a matter of fact, I cannot get enough affection.

A second part of the training is to be able to sit very still for a long period of time. Even though I love activity and exercise, the job of a therapy dog is to not startle a person who is sick or make a commotion in the hospital, which is a quiet place. The patient is supposed to be soothed by my presence and by being able to touch me. I can do this because it makes me feel very good to bring comfort to a person. I also know that when I go home, I will take a long walk or get to play with my "fursisters" in the backyard. So, I will get all the exercise I need. Best of all, my mom will be proud of me and tell me what a good boy I am.

Another thing I am learning to do is look at food on the floor or in my mom's hand and not take it until I get permission. This is really hard, especially since I was once starved, but I'm becoming good at it. This skill is important because in hospitals, all kinds of things end up on the floor, and most of them are not good for dogs or humans. I have learned to just leave those things where they are until my mom actually hands me the item if it's something I'm allowed to have.

There is more training to come, but I have to learn one thing at a time. If I excel at being a Therapy Touch dog, there is another kind of therapy training I will be able to do. I could become a "reading dog."

When I first heard that, I thought I would have to learn to read, but that's not what it's all about! A reading dog's job is to sit with children while they read out loud. It's a very important job because the children know I will love them even if they don't read well or make a mistake. I will just listen and will not judge or criticize the children. For many youngsters, this is a gift. They feel very safe reading to a dog, because we love unconditionally and we are very support-ive of children learning to read. Perhaps one day, when they feel really comfortable reading to me, they will be ready to read to their teach-ers, their parents and even other children.

Living The Good Life

I know how lucky I am to have found my "furever" family, lucky to have parents who love me and "fursisters" to play with, and best of all, lucky to be training for a very important job. I know I'm lucky because I'm no longer afraid of people. Many dogs that start out as I did never fully recover and live the happy life I do. Initially, my life was saved by Dr. Mark at the Grady Animal Hospital and then I was rescued by Craig, the best foster parent any dog could ever have. Now, I not only have a home and a "furever" family, but I also have a future that allows me to help people who need someone to love them and be there for them.

What I've Learned

No matter how unfortunate life starts out, that's only the beginning of the story, not the end. My mom and I decided that we were going to turn my history of abuse into a force for good. The man who abandoned me on someone's lawn, leaving me to die, could not have dreamed how my life would turn out. He would never know that I would be the one to let the world know about the horror of animal abuse and the wonder and power of the pet rescue world. It takes a team of dedicated people to save even one dog. Imagine how many people we need to save the MILLIONS of dogs that are waiting in shelters and rescues.

Forgiveness

While I forgive my abuser, I am determined to let the world know animal abuse still exists and together we must end the madness. Forgiveness does not change the past, it changes the future.

"I forgive you not for you, but for me. Because like chains shackling me to the past, I will no longer pollute my heart with bitterness, fear, distrust or anger. I forgive you because hate is just another way of holding on, and you don't belong here anymore."

—Beau Taplin, "Forgiveness"

There is so much work to be done and with your help we can change the future for countless homeless dogs. Will you step up and help us?

—D'Angelo

What D'Angelo Would Like Readers To Know

Why Pit Bulls Have A Bad Reputation

Many of the dogs living at the New York Bully Crew are purebred pit bulls or pit-bull mixes. It's unfortunate that we don't have a very respectable reputation. Most people still think pit bulls are mean and dangerous because they see news stories about dogfights or even attacks on people.

What they may not know is that dogs are not born mean or angry, but can become this way if we are mistreated or trained to fight. There are no bad dogs, only bad dog owners and I know this from personal experience. Most of the dogs that arrived at the New York Bully Crew had been abused, abandoned, or neglected and were in bad physical shape. I know that with the right people and help, we can change our lives. We can be "rehabilitated" (restored to our real selves) if we are given discipline, exercise, and love, either in a shelter, a foster home, or a "furever" home. We can become loving companions, protectors of children, and special service dogs who help people with illnesses or disabilities. Our nature is both loving and giving and I wish more people knew this about us.

Myths About Pit Bulls

- *Pit Bulls are inherently dangerous and vicious.*
  While pit bulls are a strong, powerful
  breed, they are not born mean. Like people,
  they are products of their upbringing and
  environment.

- *Stray pets are unpredictable because their past is
  unknown.* While it's true that you know noth-
  ing about the pit bull's backgrounds, you can
  tell a lot about dogs by the way they behave.
  Strays are often so appreciative and thankful
  to have a warm home and food that they are
  usually very easy to train. It just takes time,

patience and love and dedication to develop a well behaved dog. They are very motivated by food, which helps with the training.

- *Owning multiple dogs creates chaos and stress.* It is actually healthier for dogs to be part of a pack, as they were in the early days of civilization. A pack provides a feeling of safety, security, companionship and family.

- *An aggressive dog in a shelter should be euthanized because it is a danger to people.* Almost every dog can be rehabilitated and unlearn bad behavior. A shelter can be very stressful for a dog, especially if it was left there by its owner or it was a stray that had to fight for survival. Many dogs that seem aggressive are just nervous and frightened. With the proper care and a healthy environment, such dogs will calm down and learn to trust again.

■ *Once a dog displays aggressive tendencies, it can't be rehabilitated.* This is simply not true. With love and support, most dogs can be retrained and transformed into affectionate companions.

The best doggie love story ever.

The Truth About Pit Bulls

- Millions of dogs in shelters will be euthanized (put to sleep) due to overcrowding. This is the number one cause of death in all dogs. (dogbreedinfo.com)
- Early spaying and neutering will decrease the problem of dog overpopulation.
- Having a pet is good for your health. People who own pets live almost 4 years longer than individuals who don't own a pet.
- Even a "mean" dog can be changed and made pleasant and agreeable through exercise, discipline, and affection, in that order.

- Owning multiple pets doesn't take much more work or effort than caring for one pet, and it creates comfort and companionship for the other dogs.
- Pit bulls are not a specific breed. Many different breeds and breed mixes fall under the general "pit bull" category.
- Throughout the late 19th century and early 20th centuries, the pit bull was known as the "Nanny Dog" due to its love and devotion to children. (truthaboutpitbull.blogspot.com)

D'Angelo comforting Nestle on the couch.

Why We Should Prevent Unwanted Puppies

Some of the dogs I met at the New York Bully Crew had been forced to have many, many litters of puppies because pit bull puppies can sell for thousands of dollars. Their unlicensed owners are called backyard breeders, and sad to say, they are not responsible owners. Responsible owners would have spayed and neutered their dogs so they would not produce too many puppies. Puppies are lovable and adorable creatures, but when there are too many and some are not sold, they are often mistreated or abandoned. Sometimes, these are the dogs that end up in shelters.

The Rainbow Bridge Poem

There is a bridge connecting Heaven and Earth. It's called the Rainbow Bridge because of its many colors. Just this side of the Rainbow Bridge there is a land of hills, meadows and valleys with lush green grass.

When a beloved pet dies, it goes to this special place where there is food and water and warm spring weather. It is a beautiful and spectacular place.

Old and frail animals become young again. Those who are injured are made whole again, and they are just as we remembered them. They play all day with each other. There is only one thing missing. They are not with the special people who loved them on earth.

These animals run and play until the day comes when one suddenly stops playing and looks up! Its nose twitches! Its ears perk up! Its eyes begin to stare! And then it suddenly runs from the group!

You have been seen and when you and your special friend meet, you take your pet in your arms and embrace. Your face is kissed again and again and you look once more into the eyes of your trusting pet. Then you cross the Rainbow Bridge together, never to be separated again.

—*Author unknown*

Find out more about how to adopt a pit bull at www.nybullycrew.org. You can also contact your local pet rescue. Keep up with D'Angelo at www.pitbullsuperstar.org and on Instagram @ dangelo_nybc.

D'Angelo sporting his New York Bully Crew gear.

Glossary

- **Euthanasia:** Also called "mercy killing." This is the act of putting an animal to death. This is sometimes humane due to a severe injury or incurable illness, but is also performed to curb overcrowding of shelters, or because an animal has yet to find a home.

- **Spaying and Neutering:** The removal of an animal's reproductive organs to prevent unwanted puppies. This practice helps prevent overpopulation of animals that may not be able to find a home.

- **Pet Fostering:** A critical part of animal rescue. This practice allows for the temporary housing of animals with a caregiver in a home until the animal is placed permanently with a person or a family.

- **Stereotype:** A thought or feeling that may not accurately reflect reality. Stereotypes are often used to characterize animals, people or things. Oftentimes, the label is inaccurate especially when it applies to pit bulls.

- **Backyard Breeder:** An unlicensed breeder not registered as a legitimate breeder in his state who does not necessarily comply with rules and regulations mandated by the state. Oftentimes, puppies from backyard breeders are sold for less money than those from legitimate breeders because dogs are bred without experience and knowledge and sometimes the puppies are not healthy. Not all backyard breeders are unethical, yet we still don't recommend buying a puppy from a backyard breeder. You don't know what you are buying and may end up with an unhealthy dog. Instead, we recommend rescuing a shelter dog.

- **Bait Dog:** Normally a submissive dog used by abusive people to train their fighting dogs or used to start a dog fight. The bait dog typically won't fight back. Sometimes its mouth is taped shut to prevent it from protecting itself. This is a horrific form of animal abuse.
- **Rehabilitation:** The act of recovering from neglect or abuse and being restored to our former selves.
- **Therapy Touch Dog:** A dog that visits patients or residents in a hospital or facility and allow themselves to be touched by humans. People find comfort and are often calmed by the presence of a well-tempered, well-trained therapy dog.

D'Angelo, before and after.

Big ol' pittie smile!

Happy New Year from the Pack: Nestle, D'Angelo,
Miss Piggy and Daisy.

Miss Piggy's protector.

D'Angelo butts up to Nestle.

Reunited with my angel Craig Fields.

Happy dogs with Kathy Qualy, Craig Fields and John Qualy.

D'Angelo loves his "Daddy."

Being loved by my big "Sister" Madison.

Sweet Dreams

Sweet dreams of pack walks, big healthy meals and lots of love.

Pile of pitties.

Rewarded for being a good boy!

All decked out!

Daisy's 82 pound pillow.

Sweet Miss Piggy looking shy.

D'Angelo and the Pack

Acknowledgements

Thank you to everyone involved with animal welfare and rescue all over the world. Countless animals are given a second chance thanks to your devotion and loving work. Teamwork truly saves lives and it starts with your amazing actions.

To Craig Fields—thank you for starting the Bully Crew. You have an unbelievable love and passion for saving every dog you possibly can. The endless energy you put toward changing negative perceptions about pit bulls and opening people's eyes to how amazing the breed really is, has definitely made an enormous impact in the world of rescue and will continue to do so. You are truly an inspiration! We are so grateful that you never gave up on D'Angelo, even when he was mere hours from crossing the Rainbow Bridge. You took D'Angelo into your home until he was healthy enough to come into ours, and then selflessly gave him to us after you fell in love with him yourself. Thank you for blessing us with such an amazing gift. And to everybody at New York Bully Crew—we admire and appreciate your selfless work and for being a no-kill animal rescue.

Thank you, Peggy Nehmen, for assisting with the book design and for being such a professional. To Peggy Bauer, Madison Qualy, Kira Henschel, and Jerry Skupin who helped tremendously with the editing of this important book.

To Maya Klauber, whose illustrations take us into D'Angelo's soul. You truly captured his personality with your beautiful artwork.

To our beautiful daughter Madison—thank you for discovering NYBC and asking us to help them. You are the reason we found D'Angelo. Your love for all animals is inspiring to everyone who knows you.

My deepest gratitude to my husband John for allowing me to pursue my passion for animal rescue. You have always supported my dreams and this one has become a reality. Thank you for loving our pack as much as I do, so much so that they are finally allowed in our bed.

D'Angelo, "My Lil Superstar," thank you for enduring your abuse and allowing me to use it as a force for good. May the existence of such abuse be constantly exposed so that it can be stopped in its tracks. Thank you for your determination to live, and for being the most kind-hearted doggie I have ever known. You have boosted Miss Piggy's confidence and helped her start to trust again. Thank you for making each member of our pack better—both the dogs and humans.

Finally, thank you, God, for the amazing gift of dogs and the remarkable way they touch our lives.

About The Author

Kathy Qualy has always loved animals. Her true passion for protecting their welfare was sparked at age nine when her family rescued their first dog. Today, Kathy and her husband John live in Missouri, where they share their home with three pit bulls and one beautiful black mutt. They celebrate, support, and encourage all animal rescue efforts.

About the Illustrator

Maya Klauber lives in Manhattan, New York, with her husband and two rescue beagles. She started a small business called "Water Collars," in 2015, painting custom pet portraits. She donates a portion of every sale to animal rescue, combining her two greatest passions—helping animals and creating art.

Thank you for reading my story!

Dear Miss Piggy,

Although you only walked this earth 4½ years, you filled our lives with so much love and joy our hearts ache now that you are gone. You crossed The Rainbow Bridge much too early. The love you and D'Angelo shared was truly remarkable. We are so proud of you because although you endured abuse as a puppy, you learned to trust humans and doggies again with D'Angelo at your side giving you the confidence you needed. You were the perfect itty-bitty blue-nosed pocket Pittie. We are so blessed you were a part of our family and we promise to never forget you. RIP Miss Piggy, 10/2011 – 7/11/2016.

Love forever,
Your Qualy Pack